Healthy Arms, Happy Kids

An Easy to Follow Guide to Preventing Arm Injuries in Children Ages 6-12

WALTER A. BEEDE

Copyright © 2023 Beede Baseball Publishing LLC

All rights reserved. No part of this book may be reproduced or transmitted in any form or by any means, electronic or mechanical, including photocopying, recording, or by an information storage and retrieval system—except by a reviewer who may quote brief passages in a review—without permission in writing from the publisher.

Beede Baseball Publishing LLC

Lynn MA 01902

https://www.baseballprocess.com

CONTENTS

Arm Care 1

The Mound Versus Flat Ground 5

Throwing Different Types of Balls 9

The Importance of Warmups and Cooldowns 14

Understanding Why Injuries Have Increased 23

Warning Signs 25

What Can You Do? 28

About the Author 32

Arm Care

Arm injuries in youth baseball are a growing concern that affects players, coaches, and parents alike. These injuries can vary from minor strains to more severe conditions, such as ulnar collateral ligament (UCL) tears that require surgery. Addressing arm injuries in youth baseball is crucial as they can have long-term effects on a player's performance and overall health.

Overuse injuries are common in youth baseball, particularly in the shoulder and elbow, caused by repeatedly performing the same motion that leads to stress on the affected area. The repetitive movements involved in baseball throwing can be particularly harmful if players do not get enough rest and recovery time. Common causes of overuse injuries include throwing too much or too hard too soon, poor posture, improper warmup and stretching, and poor throwing mechanics.

Ways to prevent and treat overuse injuries include a gradual increase in the amount and intensity of throwing, proper warmup and stretching, adequate rest and recovery time between throwing sessions, regular strength and conditioning exercises, and using proper throwing mechanics.

Proper throwing mechanics are essential for preventing arm injuries in youth baseball; poor mechanics put additional stress on the shoulder and elbow. Common problems include poor posture, lack of follow-through, and needing to use the legs more during the throw. Tips for improving throwing mechanics include:

- Practicing proper posture.
- Focusing on a smooth and fluid throwing motion.
- Incorporating the legs into the throw.
- Practicing with lighter balls before moving on to heavier balls.

Strength and conditioning are essential in preventing arm injuries in youth baseball. Stronger and more flexible players are less likely to suffer from overuse injuries. Recommendations for strength and conditioning exercises include resistance band exercises for the shoulder and elbow, core strengthening exercises, and dynamic stretching and foam rolling to improve flexibility. It is important to remember that proper progression and load management are essential in strength and conditioning. Players should start with lighter weights and gradually increase the intensity of their exercises. Young athletes that use progression-based strength programs to help prevent injury will ensure that the player is making progress safely and effectively.

Warmup and stretching are crucial for preventing arm injuries in youth baseball. A proper warmup helps to prepare the muscles for the demands of throwing, while stretching helps to improve flexibility and reduce the risk of injury. Recommended warmup and stretching routines include dynamic stretching to warm up the muscles, stretching the shoulder, elbow, and wrist to improve flexibility, and incorporating foam rolling into the warmup and stretching routine to improve mobility and reduce the risk of injury.

Playing on poorly maintained fields can also increase the risk of injury in youth baseball. Some of the risks could be better maintained playing surfaces, equipment, lighting, and better weather conditions. You can reduce these risks by mowing the grass, maintaining the proper moisture level in the field, regularly checking and repairing damaged equipment, and providing adequate lighting for night games and practices. Regarding weather, periodically check the weather forecast and postpone games or practices if necessary.

Proper equipment is essential for preventing arm injuries in youth baseball because the wrong equipment can increase the risk of injury and negatively impact a player's performance on the field. Therefore, choose gloves and cleats that fit correctly and provide adequate support, use balls and bats that are the appropriate weight for the player's age and skill level, and regularly check equipment and replace it if it is damaged or worn out.

Arm injuries in youth baseball are a serious concern that parents should address and monitor. The tips in this chapter are a foundation. By following the recommendations outlined in this book, parents, coaches, and players can work together to prevent arm injuries and ensure a safe and enjoyable experience for all involved.

The Mound Versus Flat Ground

Throwing a baseball from a pitching mound causes more stress on the arm and body than on a flat surface for several reasons. In this chapter, we will explore the biomechanics of pitching and how the elevated mound affects the pitcher's movements and puts more stress on the arm and body.

When pitchers throw from a flat surface, their body weight is evenly distributed between their feet. However, the pitching mound is elevated 10 inches above the level of home plate. When pitching from a mound, the pitcher's body weight shifts forward and downward, creating additional stress on the front of the shoulder and elbow. This other downward force generated by the pitcher's body weight is one of the biggest challenges of pitching from a mound. It can increase the risk of injury, particularly in rotator cuff tears, labral tears, and elbow ligament injuries.

Another factor contributing to the increased pitching stress from a mound is the altered biomechanics of the pitcher's delivery. The pitcher's arm and body move more straightforwardly and linearly when pitching from a flat surface. However, when pitching from a mound, the pitcher must make additional adjustments to their delivery to compensate for the elevated surface. Throwing from that high surface can result in altered biomechanics, which can put more stress on the arm and body. For example, pitching from a mound requires the pitcher to generate more force to overcome the downward slope, leading to increased upper body and arm strength, which can cause injury. Additionally, the pitcher must adjust their landing position due to the slope of the mound, causing increased stress on the knees and lower back, which can result in knee and back injuries.

One of the critical ways the elevated mound affects the pitcher's delivery is through the altered angle of their arm slot. When pitching from a flat surface, the pitcher's arm is typically in a neutral position, with the elbow at a 90-degree angle and the arm in a straight line with the shoulder. However, when pitching from a mound, the arm must be raised higher to overcome the downward slope. This altered arm slot can result in increased stress on the shoulder, as well as increased strain on the elbow and wrist.

Another factor contributing to the increased pitching stress from a mound is the altered timing of the pitcher's delivery. When pitching from a flat surface, the pitcher has a more consistent delivery timing, with the arm and body moving in a smooth and coordinated motion. However, when pitching from a mound, the pitcher must adjust their timing to compensate for the slope. The height of the pitching mound can result in an altered timing of the pitcher's delivery, putting more stress on the arm and body.

In addition to the physical demands of pitching from a mound, psychological factors contribute to the increased stress. For some pitchers, the elevated surface can be intimidating and make them feel as though they are under more pressure to perform. The spotlight of the pitcher's mound can increase anxiety and stress, negatively impacting their performance and increasing the risk of injury.

Let's review. Throwing a baseball from a pitching mound causes more stress on the arm and body than pitching on a flat surface due to the additional downward force generated by the pitcher's body weight, the altered biomechanics of the pitcher's delivery, the modified angle of their arm slot, the adjusted timing of their delivery, and the psychological pressure that comes with pitching from an elevated surface. These factors contribute to an increased risk of injury for the pitcher, particularly in the form of rotator cuff tears, labral tears, elbow ligament injuries, knee injuries, and back injuries. Therefore, pitchers must be aware of these risks.

Throwing Different Types of Balls

Throwing a variety of balls at younger ages can help promote arm health and strength. The benefits start with various stress on muscles. Throwing different types of balls can stress other muscles in the arm and shoulder, which can help prevent overuse injuries. For example, throwing a heavier ball, such as a softball, can strengthen the muscles that stabilize the shoulder, while throwing a lighter ball, like a tennis ball, can help to build speed and endurance in the arm muscles.

Here are some other benefits.

- Improved coordination: Throwing different types of balls can improve coordination and balance. For example, throwing a smaller ball like a lacrosse ball or a Wiffle ball requires greater precision and control, which can translate to better accuracy when throwing a baseball.

- Enhanced strength and power: Throwing heavier balls can improve overall arm strength and power. For example, throwing a heavy medicine ball or weighted baseball can help increase arm and shoulder strength, translating to greater velocity when throwing a baseball.

- Reduced boredom and monotony: Mixing up throwing routines with different types of balls can also add variety to a training program. Variety can make training more enjoyable and sustainable in the long term.

- Injury prevention: Finally, throwing different types of balls can help to prevent injuries by reducing the overall stress on the arm and shoulder. By incorporating various throwing exercises and drills, young athletes can reduce the risk of overuse injuries and maintain their arm health and strength.

However, one type of ball tends to stand above the rest: a football. Throwing a football can help young baseball players improve their arm health and strength. Here is how. The motion of throwing a football requires the athlete to use the same muscles as throwing a baseball. However, the weight and size of a football are generally more than that of a baseball, which means that young athletes can work on building up their arm strength and on allowing the body to get more involved. Throwing a football is a great way to build strength in the arm, shoulder, and back muscles. By building up their arm strength through throwing a football, young baseball players can prevent injury and improve their performance on the field.

Secondly, throwing a football can help young baseball players improve their throwing mechanics. Throwing a football requires a different throwing motion than throwing a baseball, but the principles of good throwing mechanics are the same. Athletes must keep their elbows at shoulder height and their wrists straight and relaxed when throwing a football; these principles are essential for throwing a baseball. Throwing a football also promotes an efficient arm path and allows the arm to pronate, which helps protect the elbow naturally. How many quarterbacks have you heard of that needed Tommy John surgery versus baseball players? By practicing good throwing mechanics while throwing a football, young baseball players can develop better muscle memory and improve their accuracy and velocity when throwing a baseball.

Throwing a football can also help young baseball players prevent arm fatigue. Throwing a baseball can put a lot of stress on the arm and shoulder muscles, especially if done too frequently and without proper rest and recovery time. By alternating between throwing a football and throwing a baseball, young athletes can reduce the stress on their arm muscles while still maintaining their throwing abilities. Maintaining consistent throwing routines can help prevent arm fatigue and reduce the risk of injury.

Lastly, throwing a football can help young baseball players develop mental toughness. Throwing a football will help with accuracy as young athletes have a bigger target to throw to. Football is a sport that requires a lot of mental toughness and focus, especially for the quarterback position. By throwing a football daily, young athletes can improve their ability to focus and maintain concentration for extended periods. This mental toughness can translate to improved performance on the baseball field, where the ability to stay focused and perform under pressure is crucial.

In conclusion, throwing different types of balls can provide several benefits for building arm health and strength. By incorporating various throwing exercises into a training program, young athletes can reduce the risk of overuse injuries, improve coordination and balance, and increase overall arm strength and power. Throwing a football can further help young baseball players looking to improve their arm health and strength. By building their strength, enhancing their throwing mechanics, preventing arm fatigue, and developing mental toughness, young athletes can become better baseball players and reduce their risk of injury. As with any training program, it's essential to start slowly and gradually increase the amount and intensity of the training. With proper training and guidance, young athletes can benefit significantly from incorporating football throwing into their daily routine.

The Importance of Warmups and Cooldowns

Warmups and cooldowns are essential components of any exercise or training routine. A proper warmup should prepare the body for the demands of the activity, while a cooldown helps to return the body to a relaxed state after exercise. Athletes of all ages, especially young throwing athletes, must take extra care when it comes to warming up and cooling down to avoid injury and achieve peak performance. This chapter will discuss the importance of warmups and cooldowns for young throwing athletes and how to incorporate them into a training regimen.

Warming Up

A warmup is a crucial component of any physical activity. It helps to increase heart rate, blood flow, and oxygen delivery to the muscles, preparing them for the movement's demands. A proper warmup can also help to reduce the risk of injury by increasing the flexibility of the muscles and joints, improving the range of motion, and reducing the risk of muscle strains and tears. An example of a proper warmup exercise for throwing a baseball is the arm circles exercise. Arm circles are a great warmup exercise for throwing a baseball because they help to increase blood flow to the shoulders and upper back, improve the range of motion, and activate the muscles used in pitching. Here is how to perform it:

1. Stand with your feet shoulder-width apart and your arms at your sides.
2. Slowly raise your arms to your sides and make small circles with your arms.
3. Gradually increase the circles' size until your arms make large circles.
4. Continue making the circles for 10–15 seconds, then reverse the direction of the circles and make them in the opposite direction for another 10–15 seconds.
5. Repeat the exercise for 2–3 sets, gradually increasing the speed and size of the circles as you go.

A more targeted exercise is the shoulder rotation. To perform a shoulder rotation, the individual stands with arms relaxed at their sides and slowly raises them to shoulder height. Then, rotate the arms forward or backward in a circular motion. This exercise explicitly targets the shoulder joint and can be used to improve mobility, flexibility, and range of motion in the shoulder. The main difference between arm and shoulder rotations is that arm circles are a more general exercise involving more significant movements of the entire arm. In contrast, shoulder rotations are a more focused exercise targeting the shoulder joint. While both exercises can be used as warmup exercises before physical activity, shoulder rotations are often used as therapeutic exercises to help improve shoulder mobility and flexibility.

In general, arm circles and shoulder rotations can be beneficial exercises for maintaining shoulder health and preventing injury. It's essential to perform these exercises correctly and gradually increase the intensity and range of motion over time to avoid injury. Additionally, if an individual has any pre-existing shoulder conditions or injuries, they should consult a healthcare professional before performing these exercises to ensure they are safe and appropriate.

Other exercises that benefit younger athletes in a warmup routine for throwing a baseball include triceps stretches and light jogging or jumping jacks to increase the heart rate and warm up the entire body. It's important to gradually increase the intensity of the warmup exercises to avoid injury and prepare the body for the demands of throwing a baseball.

Warming up is especially important for young throwing athletes because of the repetitive and high-intensity nature of throwing activities. Throwing requires a lot of power and explosive movements, which can strain muscles and joints significantly. A proper warmup can help to prepare the body for the demands of throwing by increasing blood flow to the muscles, improving flexibility, and enhancing coordination.

A proper warmup for young throwing athletes should include dynamic stretching, which involves moving the joints through their full range of motion in a controlled manner. These exercises can help to increase blood flow, improve range of motion, and activate the muscles used in throwing. It is essential to perform a dynamic warmup routine before throwing, which means exercises that involve movement and gradually increasing intensity. This warmup will help prepare the body for the demands of throwing and reduce the risk of injury.

Here are five examples of warmup exercises for young throwing athletes. Parents of young throwing athletes can do this with their athletes to show proper movements:

1. **Arm circles**: As described above, arm circles are a great way to warm up the shoulders and activate the muscles used in throwing.

2. **Shoulder rotations**: Stand with your arms at your sides and your feet shoulder-width apart. Slowly raise your arms to your sides and bring them to shoulder height, then rotate them in small circles. Gradually increase the size of the circles and repeat for 10–15 seconds, then reverse the direction of the circles and repeat.

3. **Hip rotations**: Stand with your feet shoulder-width apart and your hands on your hips. Slowly rotate your hips in a circle, bringing them forward, to the side, back, and then to the other side. Repeat for 10–15 seconds, then reverse the direction of the circles and repeat.

4. **Lunges**: Step forward with one foot and bend your knee to create a lunge position with your other foot behind you. Hold the place for a few seconds, then push back up to the starting position. Repeat with the other leg and continue for 10–15 reps.

5. **Jumping jacks**: Stand with your feet together and your arms at your sides. Jump up and spread your legs to the sides while raising your arms overhead. Jump again to bring your feet back together and lower your arms. Repeat for 10–15 reps.

Cooling Down

After exercising or engaging in sports practice, it's crucial to cool down the body to restore it to a relaxed state. Proper cooldown methods can reduce the likelihood of injury, prevent muscle soreness, and facilitate recovery. Moreover, cooling down can lower the heart rate and blood pressure, reducing the risk of dizziness and other post-workout symptoms.

For young athletes involved in throwing sports, cooling down is especially important. Throwing involves powerful and explosive movements that can cause muscle soreness and fatigue. A proper cooldown routine can reduce or prevent these effects and promote recovery, enabling young athletes to perform their best during subsequent practice or games.

Static stretching, which involves holding a stretch without movement, should be part of the cooldown routine. An example is the hamstring stretch, which is performed as follows:

1. Sit on the ground with your legs straight out.
2. Slowly reach forward and try to touch your toes with your fingers.
3. Hold the stretch for 10–30 seconds, and you should feel a gentle stretch in the back of your legs.

4. If you cannot reach your toes, go as far as possible without causing pain or discomfort.
5. Slowly release the stretch and return to the starting position.

You can repeat the stretch a few times and perform it with one leg at a time by bending one knee and stretching the other leg. Static stretching is a great way to improve flexibility, reduce muscle soreness, and promote recovery after exercise.

Other components of a proper cool down for young throwing athletes may include light cardiovascular exercise, such as walking or jogging, and specific exercises that target the muscles used in throwing, such as shoulder rotations and arm swings. You may also perform static stretching exercises that target the muscles used in pitching. For example, stretching the triceps, chest, and back muscles can help to reduce muscle soreness and promote recovery. Foam rolling is another exercise; it can help release muscle tension and improve flexibility. Here are five examples of proper cooldown exercises for young throwing athletes:

1. **Shoulder stretches**: Stand with your feet shoulder-width apart and your arms at your sides. Slowly raise one arm and bring it across your chest, using your other arm to pull it closer to your body gently.

Hold the stretch for 10-15 seconds, then switch arms and repeat.

2. **Triceps stretches**: Stand with your feet shoulder-width apart and raise one arm overhead. Bend your elbow and place your hand behind your head. Use your other hand to gently pull your elbow back, feeling the stretch in your triceps. Hold for 10-15 seconds, then switch arms and repeat.

3. **Wall push-ups**: Stand facing a wall with your arms out in front of you at shoulder height. Lean forward and place your hands on the wall. Slowly lower your chest towards the wall, then push back up. Repeat for 10-15 reps.

4. **Light jogging**: Jogging or light running for a few minutes can be an excellent way to promote recovery.

5. **Foam rolling**: Use a foam roller to target the muscles used in throwing, such as the shoulders and upper back. Roll slowly back and forth over the muscles for 1-2 minutes at a time.

Incorporating Warmups and Cooldowns into a Training Regimen

Young throwing athletes should regularly incorporate warmups and cooldowns into their training regimen to maximize the benefits of warmups and cooldowns. A proper warmup should be completed before every practice or game, while a cooldown should be completed afterward. Athletes should work with their coaches or trainers to develop a routine tailored to their needs, considering their age, fitness level, and sports demands. By doing so, they can help to ensure their safety and performance during their sports activities and establish healthy habits for their future physical activity.

Understanding Why Injuries Have Increased

Over the past few decades, there has been a significant increase in arm injuries among six- to twelve-year-old baseball and softball players. Here are some of the reasons why.

Changes in the Game

One of the main reasons for increased arm injuries among children playing baseball or softball is changes in the game itself. In recent years, there has been an emphasis on faster pitches and higher velocities, leading to more stress on the arm.

Overuse

One of the most common causes of arm injuries in young baseball and softball players is overuse, including inadequate rest and recovery. Children who throw frequently or participate in too many games or practices without adequate rest can develop overuse injuries such as tendonitis, bursitis, or stress fractures. The increase in games and tournaments contributes to this, increasing opportunities for overuse injuries.

Year-Round Play

Another factor contributing to increased arm injuries is the rise of year-round play. Many young athletes now play baseball or softball all year. Year-round competition can lead to chronic pain and long-term damage even when following rest and recovery guidelines.

Age-Inappropriate Pitch Counts

Finally, due to the increased length of the season, young players are now being asked to throw more pitches at a younger age than in the past, and This can lead to overuse injuries because young players may need more strength or endurance to handle the demands of pitching at such a young age.

Warning Signs

Parents, coaches, and young players must know the warning signs of arm injuries in this age group to prevent long-term damage. Knowing the warning signs can help parents and coaches identify injuries early on, allowing for proper treatment and prevention of long-term complications.

Pain or discomfort in the arm or shoulder

One of the most common warning signs of an arm injury in young baseball and softball players is pain or discomfort in the arm or shoulder. If a child complains of persistent pain, especially when throwing or pitching, it could indicate an injury.

It's also essential to pay attention to the location of the pain. For instance, the pain in the shoulder could be a sign of rotator cuff strain or impingement. Pain in the elbow could indicate a problem with the UCL (ulnar collateral ligament) or a bone-related injury.

Decreased range of motion

Another warning sign of arm injury is decreased range of motion in the arm or shoulder. A child who experiences stiffness or difficulty moving their arm could have a muscle strain, tendonitis, or a ligament injury. Loss of range of motion can be especially prevalent in the shoulder joint, where the rotator cuff muscles play a crucial role in arm movement.

Swelling or inflammation

Swelling and inflammation around the elbow or shoulder joint are warning signs of an arm injury, so if a child experiences noticeable swelling or redness in the area could indicate an acute injury such as a fracture, dislocation, or ligament sprain.

Inflammation can also develop gradually over time due to repetitive stress on the arm. For example, repetitive throwing in baseball or softball can cause inflammation in the shoulder joint over time, leading to chronic pain and stiffness.

Weakness or numbness

Weakness or numbness in the arm or hand can also be a warning sign of an arm injury. These symptoms could indicate nerve compression or a pinched nerve, which can occur due to repeated throwing motions or sudden impact.

If a child experiences weakness or numbness in their arm or hand, they may have difficulty gripping a ball or other objects, significantly impacting their performance on the field.

Fatigue or Decreased Performance

Finally, if a child experiences unusual fatigue or decreased performance, it could indicate an arm injury. Children who typically throw with speed and accuracy may suddenly struggle to maintain their previous level of performance, suggesting an underlying issue.

Fatigue can also develop over time as the arm becomes fatigued due to repeated throwing motions. A common symptom of arm fatigue is when a young pitcher feels pain in the bicep. In these cases, children may experience decreased performance in games or practice, indicating a need for rest and recovery.

A sign of leg fatigue is when a pitcher consistently is missing high, which means his legs are tired and he has lost drive in his lower half. Young pitchers may also start to catapult or carry the ball when their legs tire and that causes them to miss high and in on their arm side.

What Can You Do?

While it's essential to recognize the warning signs of arm injuries in children, prevention is the best approach. We've already mentioned that parents, coaches, and young players can take several steps to minimize the risk of arm injuries.

Age-Appropriate Pitch Counts

Young pitchers should follow age-appropriate pitch count guidelines to prevent overuse injuries. The American Sports Medicine Institute recommends that children aged nine through twelve pitch no more than seventy-five pitches per game and no more than 600 pitches per season. Pitch Smart guidelines, developed by USA Baseball and MLB, recommend a max of fifty pitches in a game for kids under eight years old and no more than sixty combined innings in twelve months. You can find these guidelines by searching for "smart pitch guidelines" online.

Adequate Rest and Recovery Time

Young players should be allowed adequate time to rest and recover between games or practice sessions. Overuse injuries can occur when young players do not take the proper time to recover, leading to chronic pain and long-term damage. Pitch Smart is the resource here, too. Parents must know the recommended rest times and advocate for their players. Not all coaches know about Pitch Smart or follow the guidelines.

Cross-Training and Conditioning

I mentioned earlier that cross-training and conditioning can help young players build strength and endurance, reducing the risk of arm injuries. At ages six through twelve, cross-training can mean playing different sports in different seasons.

Keep conditioning work fun and age appropriate. At younger ages, this can come from playing on playground equipment, climbing trees and rocks, swinging across monkey bars, and playing touch football, pickle, or group tag games with friends (quickly starting, stopping, and changing direction builds explosiveness). At around twelve, a formal strength and conditioning program is more appropriate. I cover this in detail in my book *The Process* (2nd edition or later). Focus on exercises that target the upper body, including the shoulders, triceps, and biceps, as well as the core and lower body.

Encourage proper throwing mechanics.

It is worth repeating the point about proper throwing mechanics. My childhood coach and mentor, Jim Curtin, used to say, "Repetitions lead to retention." Teach young players to use appropriate throwing mechanics, such as keeping their elbow above their shoulder, rotating their hips, and keeping their arms close to their bodies. When young athletes focus on these proper mechanics, it will help reduce stress on the elbow and shoulder, reducing the risk of injury.

Promote good nutrition.

Good nutrition is vital for overall health and can help reduce the risk of arm injuries. Encourage young players to eat a well-balanced diet, including plenty of fruits and vegetables, whole grains, lean proteins, and healthy fats.

Avoid playing through pain.

If a young player experiences pain while playing, they should be encouraged to stop and rest. Continuing to play through pain can lead to more severe injuries and could negatively impact their long-term health and performance.

Seek medical attention.

If a young player experiences pain or discomfort while playing, they should be evaluated by a healthcare professional as soon as possible. Early intervention can help reduce the risk of more serious injuries and get the player back on the field faster.

All parents need to understand that your child is not a character from a video game. There is no such thing as a rubber arm. Often, children will not want to upset their parents or coaches, so they will try to pitch through pain. Tell them it is okay to stop if they feel pain. As parents, we must set guidelines for our children to follow. It is okay to monitor pitch counts and innings pitched. Open lines of communication between parents and youth programs ensure that children will pitch on proper rest and under appropriate pitch counts. Ensuring that our children are well-rounded and participating in various physical activities over the course of a year will ensure that your children will develop multiple physical skill sets and avoid overuse. For many teenagers, most arm injuries begin at a younger age. Always speak up when they feel tired or sore. You must be a voice for your child.

About the Author

Walter Beede

With a baseball career of over forty years, Walter Beede brings a diverse background to parents and student-athletes. His highlights as an athlete include being an All-New England First Team high school player. He received a scholarship from Arizona State University and was selected in Round 13 of the 1981 MLB draft by the Chicago Cubs. He has been a head coach at the high school, American Legion, National Travel Baseball, and NCAA levels. He has also worked as a Task Force member for the prestigious Team USA program in Cary, NC.

The parent of two sons who competed and graduated at the college level, Walter has been through the recruiting process with both of his sons, Kyle and Tyler. Kyle played for LSU Eunice and LSU Alexandria, and Tyler played for the National Champion Vanderbilt Commodores. Tyler is the only New England player in the fifty-seven-year history of the MLB draft to be a two-time, first-round selection.

Drawing from his experiences as a player, evaluator, head coach, and parent, Walter helps student-athletes and families navigate the challenges of amateur baseball—from the playing season and the recruiting process to athlete evaluations. Walter has helped more than 700 athletes from across the country over the last twenty-five years and has developed an extensive coaching and MLB scout network.

www.ingramcontent.com/pod-product-compliance
Lightning Source LLC
Chambersburg PA
CBHW070048070426
42449CB00012BA/3189